Jewelry Findings

Clamshell Bead Tip	Lobster Claw Clasp	Toggle Clasp	Barrel Clasp
Jump Ring	Crimp Bead	Head Pin	Eye Pin

As bright as a bowl full of Christmas sugar candy, these bracelets are a bead lover's delight!

by Carole Rodgers

Three Bracelets - MATERIALS: Gold lobster claw clasp and tag • 2 Gold split rings or jump rings • 2 Gold clamshell bead tips • Waste seed beads • Heavy Black beading thread • Size #10 beading needle • Round-nose pliers • Scissors • Bead sorting dish • Gem-Tac permanent adhesive

TIPS: Measure wrist and make beaded part of bracelet 1" less than measurement. You may need to add or subtract beads for the correct length. Thread needle with 24" of thread and tie a waste seed bead securely to end. Pass needle through clamshell tip from inside, glue waste bead and cut off excess thread (see page 15). Carefully close clamshell. To finish bracelet, pick up clamshell and tie off thread against a waste bead, glue, trim and close. Make loop in shank of clamshell. Attach clamshells to split rings and rings to clasp and tag.

BROWN BRACELET - MATERIALS: 14 to 16 White 6mm beads • 16 to 18 Root Beer E beads • Large Brown bead
Start with Brown E bead and alternate with White for first half of bracelet. Add large bead and finish other side.

RED BRACELET - MATERIALS: 12 to 14 White 6mm beads • 10 to 12 Red 6mm square beads • Large Red bead
Alternately thread 6 White and 5 Red beads. Add large Red bead and finish other side of bracelet.

MULTI BRACELET - MATERIALS: 7 glass tube beads • 8 Black 6mm beads
Alternately thread Black and tube beads.

Attach Clasp

1. Thread crimp bead and clasp on wire. Go back through crimp bead.

2. Move bead close to clasp. Flatten crimp bead into a C shape.

3. Round crimp bead with end of pliers.

Basic Instructions Index

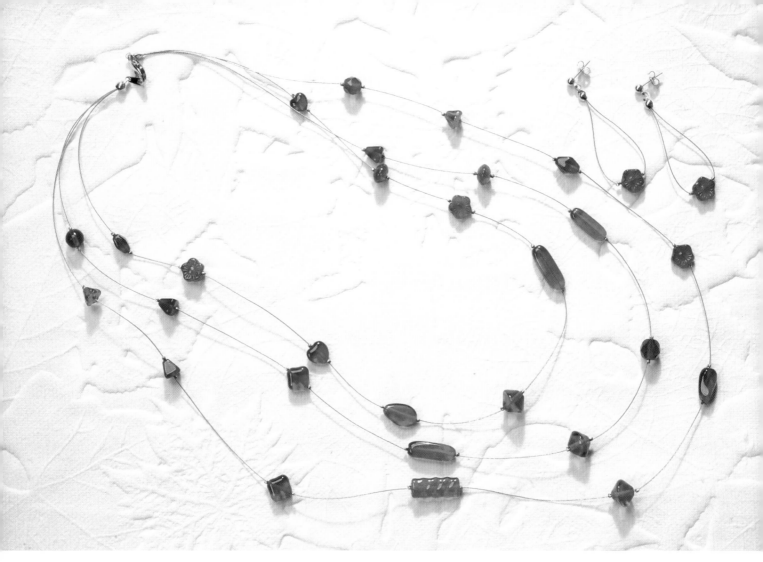

illuSion Beading

Jewel red beads almost seem to float on air in a delicate neck-lace anyone would love to own!

by Carole Rodgers

Red Illusion - MATERIALS: Red Assortment glass beads • 81" of Beadalon Gold 19-strand beading wire • Gold crimp beads • Gold lobster claw clasp and tag • 4 Gold clamshell bead tips • Gold ball and loop earrings • Crimp pliers • Wire cutters • Needle-nose pliers • Round-nose pliers • Bead sorting dish

TIPS: Cut 30", 25", 20" and two 3" pieces of wire. Pour beads into dish and pick out 3 matching beads for centers of strands. Pick out 2 for the earrings.

To make earrings, place Gold crimp bead on 3" piece of wire followed by a Red bead and another crimp bead. Be sure Red bead is in the center and close crimp beads with pliers. Place ends of wire together and slip through clamshell tip from the bottom. Place crimp bead over ends about ⅛" down from end and crimp in place. (If you do not have crimp pliers, flatten crimps with needle-nose pliers then fold bead in half again around wire.) Trim ends of wire. Close clamshell. Bend loop in clamshell shank and attach to earring. Repeat to make other earring.

For necklace, place center bead on 20" wire, place crimp bead on either side and close crimp. Randomly crimp 4 more beads on either side of center. Repeat with 25" wire using 4 beads on each side. On 30" wire, use 4 or 5 beads on each side. Place wire ends together through clamshell and crimp bead. Crimp to secure. Trim wire and close clamshell. Repeat for other side. Bend loops in shanks of clamshells and attach to clasp and tag.

Attach Crimp Bead

1. Thread crimp bead on end of wire.

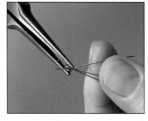

2. Make loop and thread wire through crimp. Flatten the crimp.

Make Earrings

Clamshell

Crimp

Gold Ball and Loop Earring

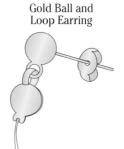

Make Necklace

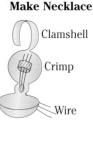

Clamshell

Crimp

Wire

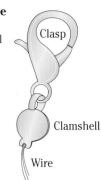

Clasp

Clamshell

Wire

Earrings and Necklace — Thread crimp bead, Red bead and crimp bead.

Necklaces & Brooches

Shimmering glass beads in various shapes and sizes dangle from rich gold and silver chains and brooches... make projects in the colors shown or choose your own!

by Carole Rodgers

Cane Glass Necklaces - YELLOW NECKLACE MATERIALS: 5 Yellow/Clear/Green Cane glass beads • 6 Gold 6mm beads • 22" Gold chain with clasp • 3" Gold eye pin • 2 Gold 4mm jump rings
MULTI NECKLACE - MATERIALS: 5 Multi-Color Cane glass beads • 6 Silver 6mm beads • 24" Silver chain with clasp • 3" Silver eye pin • 2 Silver 4mm jump rings • Wire cutters • Needle-nose pliers • Round-nose pliers
TIPS: For each necklace, thread beads on eye pin following diagram. Bend pin at right angle against last bead in same direction as loop on other end and trim to ³⁄₈". Make a loop with round-nose pliers. Be sure loops are aligned. Attach beaded pin to chain necklace with jump rings. Bend beaded pin into a slight curve upward.

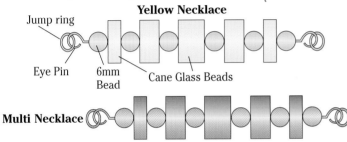

Yellow Necklace

Jump ring — Eye Pin — 6mm Bead — Cane Glass Beads

Multi Necklace

Dangle Brooches

MATERIALS: Gold 11° seed beads • Needle-nose and round-nose pliers • Wire cutters • Bead sorting dish
CRYSTAL BROOCH - MATERIALS: Crystal Assortment glass beads • Gold 5-dangle brooch • 5 Gold 2" head pins • 5 Gold 4mm jump rings
RED BROOCH - MATERIALS: Red and Black Assortment beads • ColorCraft 22 gauge Gold wire • Large Gold safety pin brooch • 5 Gold 4mm jump rings
TIPS: For Red Brooch, sort Red and Black beads for each of the 5 dangles. The dangles are all different lengths so you will need a variety of sizes. Cut 10" of Gold wire and straighten with fingers. Work with it very carefully to avoid marring surface. Make small loop in one end and spiral wire around loop 2 times. Refer to diagram. Thread beads chosen for one dangle alternating with Gold seed beads. If desired make another spiral part way up dangle. Finish with a closed loop or a spiral. Make 5 dangles of varying lengths. Attach to brooch with jump rings. Place the longest dangle in the center.

For Crystal Brooch, thread beads on head pins. alternating with Gold seed beads. Bend pin at a right angle and trim to ³⁄₈". Make a loop with round-nose pliers. Attach dangles on brooch with jump rings.

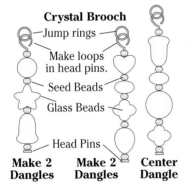

Crystal Brooch

Jump rings — Make loops in head pins. — Seed Beads — Glass Beads — Head Pins

Make 2 Dangles   **Make 2 Dangles**   **Center Dangle**

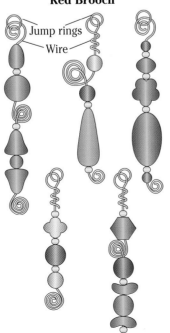

Red Brooch

Jump rings — Wire

Dangle Designs

Make an Eye Loop

1. Trim wire to ³⁄₈". Grasp end of wire with needle-nose pliers and turn at a 90° angle.

2. Grasp end of wire with round-nose pliers and roll to make a small loop.

3. Open the loop, attach and close.

Make whimsical or elegant beaded dangles and suspend them from your favorite style of necklace and earrings. Or make sweet little charms for your stemware!

by Carole Rodgers

Meow Jewelry Set - MATERIALS: 7 cat face Jet beads • 9 Black 6mm beads • 10 Black E beads • 30 Gold E beads • 14 Black 8° seed beads • Square letter beads (M, E, O, W) • Gold hoop necklace with removable ball end • 7 Gold 2" head pins • Gold ball with loop earrings • 2 Gold 4mm jump rings • Needle-nose pliers • Round-nose pliers • Wire cutters

TIPS: Make dangles on head pins following diagrams. Bend head pins at right angle just above last bead with needle-nose pliers. Trim to ³⁄₈" and make loop with round-nose pliers.

To construct necklace, remove ball end. Thread Black E, Gold E, Black E, Gold E, Black E, dangle, Gold E, letter W, Gold E, dangle, Gold E, letter O, Gold E, dangle. Reverse and repeat pattern adding E and M letter beads. Replace ball on necklace.

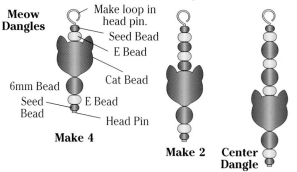

Meow Dangles

Make loop in head pin.
Seed Bead
E Bead
Cat Bead
6mm Bead
Seed Bead
E Bead
Head Pin

Make 4

Make 2

Center Dangle

Blue Dots Set - MATERIALS: 5 Blue/White/Black square dot beads • Silver fluted beads (six 5mm x 7mm, six 4mm, six 6mm fluted spacer) • Silver wire necklace with removable ball end • 2" Silver head pin • 2 Silver 30mm Silver hoops with loops • Silver ball and loop earrings • 2 Silver 4mm jump rings • Round-nose pliers • Needle-nose pliers • Wire cutters

TIPS: Necklace - On head pin, thread 4mm, 6mm, 5mm x 7mm, square, 5mm x 7mm, 6mm and 4mm beads. Bend pin at a right angle just above last bead with needle-nose pliers. Trim to ³⁄₈" and make loop with round-nose pliers. Remove ball on one end of necklace. Thread 5mm x 7mm, square, 5mm x 7mm and beaded head pin. Reverse and repeat pattern.

For earrings, thread 4mm, 6mm, square, 6mm and 4mm beads on hoop. Make a loop at end of hoop and bend to meet loop on other side. Insert jump ring in both loops and attach to earring.

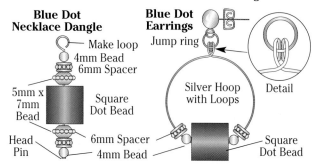

Blue Dot Necklace Dangle

Make loop
4mm Bead
6mm Spacer
5mm x 7mm Bead
Square Dot Bead
Head Pin
6mm Spacer
4mm Bead

Blue Dot Earrings

Jump ring
Silver Hoop with Loops
Detail
Square Dot Bead

by Carole Rodgers

Red & Black Ball Chain

MATERIALS: Red Assortment glass beads • Jet Assortment glass beads • 18 Silver/Black 5mm x 3mm metal drum beads • Black E beads • Black 11° seed beads • 18" Silver 4mm ball chain necklace • 9 Silver 2" head pins • 9 Silver 4mm jump rings • Silver ball and loop earring findings • Needle-nose pliers • Round-nose pliers • Wire cutters • Bead sorting dishes

TIPS: Pour Red and Black beads into separate dishes. Make dangles. Make one pin for center with largest or fanciest bead. Make all pins about the same size. Dangles have 1½" of beads. Use small Black beads at top and bottom to equalize sizes. Bend each pin at a right angle against last bead. Trim pin to ³⁄₈" and make loop at end of all 9 pins with round-nose pliers. Attach one pair of pins to earrings with jump rings.

If number of 4mm balls on chain is not equal, use wire cutters to remove one ball from end. Find center of necklace and attach center dangle with a jump ring. Continue adding dangles with jump rings referring to photo.

Earrings - Attach jump rings to head pin loops and then to ball and loop earring.

Red & Black Ball Chain Necklace Dangles

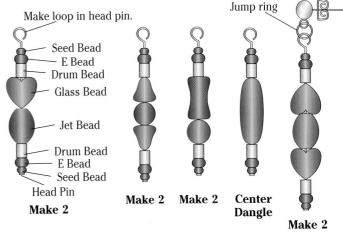

Make loop in head pin.

- Seed Bead
- E Bead
- Drum Bead
- Glass Bead
- Jet Bead
- Drum Bead
- E Bead
- Seed Bead
- Head Pin

Make 2

Jump ring

Make 2 **Make 2** **Center Dangle**

Make 2

by Carole Rodgers

Wine Glass Charms

MATERIALS: 4 pieces of ring Memory Wire • Matte Black seed beads • Assorted leftover beads • 4 Silver 13mm sun face beads • Round-nose pliers • Bead sorting dish

TIPS: Sort beads by color and find 2 of each. String a sun face on center of one piece of wire and fill sides by alternating colored and Black seed beads. Make small loop on each end with round-nose pliers. Repeat to make 3 more charms.

Multiple Strands

In this unusual necklace, amethyst beads in unique shapes are strung randomly to create a chain and smaller amethyst beads are gathered into gold bead caps for one-of-a-kind beauty!

by Carole Rodgers

Amethyst Set - MATERIALS: Amethyst Assortment glass beads • Amethyst Mini Assortment glass beads • 2 Gold 10mm bead caps • 4 Gold 4mm jump rings or split rings • 2 Gold crimp beads • Gold lobster claw clasp and tag • Gold ball and loop earrings • 2 Gold 2" head pins • Two 20" pieces of Beadalon 19-strand beading wire • Heavy White beading thread • Size #10 beading needle • Scissors • Wire cutters • Crimp Pliers • Round-nose pliers • Bead sorting dish • Tape

TIPS: For earrings, pour out larger beads and place matching beads in separate piles. You will need 2 each of 3 different beads. Thread seed beads from mini assortment on head pin alternating with larger beads until you have 3 large beads. Bend pin at a right angle and trim to 3/8". Make loop and attach to earrings with jump rings.

For necklace, fold wires so ends meet and loop in center. Tape one loop on a flat work surface. Tape second loop directly across surface 8" from first loop. Cut 90" of beading thread and single thread needle. Tie end to one loop. Pour mini beads into dish. Thread on three seed beads, then randomly string beads until you have about 7¾". Finish to 8" with seed beads. Pass needle under and over second loop. Pass needle back through 3 or 4 seed beads and begin threading beads again. Repeat process on other end being sure to pass through first few seed beads of each row. Sample has 9 strands of beads. When done, tie off thread securely on loop.

From remaining beads pick out enough pairs so that when strung with mini beads, you will have approximately 6½" on each side.

Remove tape carefully from one loop. Be sure wire ends are matched. Slip bead cap over each set of wires. Begin threading large beads alternating with seed and E beads from mini assortment. Slip on crimp bead and a split ring. Take wires back through crimp bead and 1" of beads. Close crimp with crimp pliers. Repeat for other side. Attach clasp and tag to split rings.

Amethyst Necklace

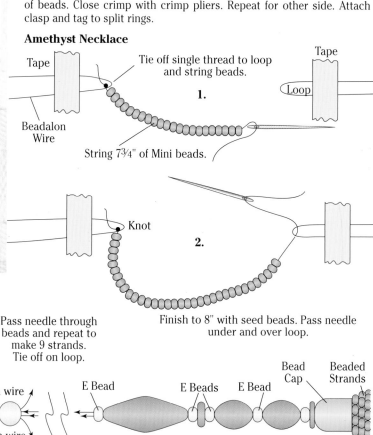

1.

Tape — Tie off single thread to loop and string beads. — Tape

Loop

Beadalon Wire

String 7¾" of Mini beads.

2.

Knot

Finish to 8" with seed beads. Pass needle under and over loop.

3.

Pass needle through.

Pass needle through.

String beads here.

Begin

Pass needle through beads and repeat to make 9 strands. Tie off on loop.

4.

Tag — Split Ring — Crimp — Trim wire — Trim wire

E Bead — E Beads — E Bead — Bead Cap — Beaded Strands

Capture memories of a clear, cool fall day with gold and brown beads and autumn toned metal leaf dangles!

by Deb Bergs

Never Enough Necklace

MATERIALS: 2 packages of Mahogany Assortment glass beads • Assorted accent seed beads • Size 6° center and 8° accent beads (Brown, Gold, Copper) • Metal leaves • Beadalon 19-strand beading wire • 24 gauge Gold wire • 14kt Gold toggle clasp • Heavy thread • Needle-nose pliers • Clear nail polish

TIPS: Lay out 12 to 14 matched pairs of glass beads and one glass bead for center. Fill in between larger beads with accent beads. Decide which bead will be the center for the swags. It should be a larger bead because several threads will pass through it. Cut 72" of thread. Tie half of clasp to one end and bead following diagrams. If you want a longer necklace, add additional sets of glass and center beads.

If your thread gets short, tie it off and start a new one.

For leaves to hang separately with a lot of movement, they need to be separated. Make small S shape Gold wire hangers. Hang one leaf on a jump ring and two without jump rings on the lower part of the S. Pinch S shut and hang from the latticework of lower part of necklace. Add as many leaf dangles as desired.

Never Enough Necklace

1. Tie clasp to one end and string beads as shown.

Clasp · Knot · E Bead · Continue beading.
2 Jump rings · Glass Bead · Accent Beads · Glass Bead

2. Continue beading to center bead.

Center Bead

3. Pass thread through last glass bead, tie knot on jump ring and return through beads to other half of clasp.

Clasp · 2 Jump rings

4. Tie off at jump ring, add nail polish to seal knot. Pass thread back through beads again and exit at first E bead. String swag beads following diagram.

Continue beading.

5. Mirror reverse at center bead and continue beading pattern to other half of clasp.

Center Bead

6. Tie off at jump ring and pass needle back through beads again and exit at first E bead. Drop down to next row and begin another swag pattern.

Continue beading.

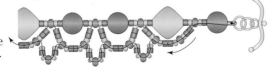

Center Bead

7. Bead swags to other end of clasp.

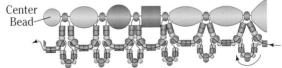

S Hook

8. Tie off at jump ring and pass thread back through row 1 and follow diagram to create last row. At center bead mirror reverse and repeat to end of clasp. Attach leaves to S Hooks.

by Carole Rodgers

Green Memory Wire Set

Green Memory Wire Set - MATERIALS: Green Assortment glass beads • 10 Silver small sun face beads • Matte Black 11° seed beads • Memory Wire (18" necklace, 18" bracelet, ring) • ColorCraft 22 gauge Black wire • Needle-nose pliers • Round-nose pliers • Bead sorting dish

TIPS: Cut memory wire to correct length by holding it with pliers and bending back and forth until it breaks. Do not use wire cutters unless especially made for memory wire as the wire will damage ordinary tools.

Ring - To make ring that is comfortable to wear, pour out beads and find smoothest ones. Make small loop in one end of ring memory wire and thread alternating Black seed beads and smooth Green beads until you have filled wire. Make small loop in end.

Necklace - To make center dangle, cut 8" of Black wire. Make small loop in one end with round-nose pliers and wrap wire around loop 5 times forming a spiral. Be sure spiral is flat. Thread several beads alternating with Black seed beads. Bend wire up about 1/8" from last bead. Make a loop and wrap wire back around 1/8". Trim wire end close. Mark center of necklace memory wire. Place wire dangle on center with a sun face bead on each side. Alternate Black seeds with Green beads for length of wire on each side. Occasionally use a sun face bead for accent. Make loops on ends to secure beads. Make 2 smaller dangles with Black wire as you did for center and hang from loops at each end.

Bracelet - To make bracelet, make a loop at one end of wire and alternately thread Black seed beads and Green beads. Occasionally thread sun face beads for accent. Make a loop on the other end. Make 2 more dangles with Black wire and hang from loops at ends of the bracelet.

Bracelet Dangles

Necklace End Dangles

Necklace Center Dangle

Make loop in wire and wrap back around about 1/8".

Make Wire Spiral

Earring

Head Pin Loop

E Beads

Glass Beads

E Bead

Head Pin

by Carole Rodgers

Amber Memory Wire Set

Amber Memory Wire Set - MATERIALS: Mahogany Assortment glass beads • 54 Root Beer E beads • 18" Memory Wire necklace • 3 Gold 2" head pins • Gold ball and loop earring findings • Bead sorting dish • Needle-nose pliers • Round-nose pliers • Super glue, optional

TIPS: Measure your neck, allow 3" for overlap and cut wire. Hold wire with pliers where you want to cut and bend back and forth until it breaks. Do not use wire cutters as the wire is very hard and will damage your tool.

Pour out beads and sort large ones. Pick out 2 sets of 3 matching beads for head pins. Use 3 large beads for center of necklace.

For earrings, thread 2 head pins as shown. Bend pin at right angle, trim to 3/8" and make a loop. Attach to earrings.

For necklace, make dangle. Then alternate E beads with large beads until you have filled both sides of wire leaving about 3/8" on each end. Use round-nose pliers to make loops.

Loop

Center Bead

Make loop in head pin.

Glass Beads

E Bead

Head Pin

Make loop at end of wire and thread beads to center bead.

Memory Wire Magic

Memory wire… what a great way to display your favorite beads in necklaces, bracelets and rings! Make matching earrings just for fun.

Cut & Bend Memory Wire

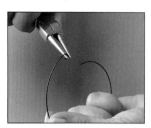

1. Hold memory wire with pliers. Bend back and forth until it breaks.

2. Make a small loop in one end of wire with round-nose pliers.

by Jennifer Mayer

Pink Charm Bracelet - MATERIALS: Pink lampwork beads • Pink Assortment glass beads • Silver barrel beads • 4 moon charms • Silver jump rings • Memory Wire bracelet • Round-nose pliers

TIPS: Use round-nose pliers to make a loop at one end of bracelet. Attach jump rings to the charms. String a medium size bead and a charm on wire. Continue adding beads in no particular pattern making sure to alternate sizes and colors of beads. String a Silver barrel bead approximately every 1" to 2" and a charm every 6". End with a charm and medium size bead. Leave approximately ¼" of memory wire and make loop.

Blue & Green Bracelet - MATERIALS: Sea Breeze Assortment glass beads • Sea Breeze Assortment mini glass beads • Silver flower dangle beads • Memory Wire bracelet • Round-nose pliers

TIPS: Use round-nose pliers to make a loop at one end of bracelet. Start with a Silver dangle bead. Add beads in no particular pattern making sure to alternate sizes and colors of beads. String a Silver dangle bead approximately every 1½". The last bead should be a Silver dangle bead. Leave approximately ¼" of memory wire and make loop.

Open & Close Jump Ring

1. Hold the jump ring on each side of the opening, rotate one pair of pliers to the side.

2. Rotate toward opening to close.

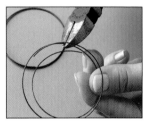

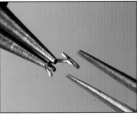

Wire Curly-Cue

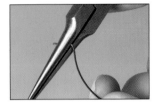

1. Bend 20 gauge wire at a 90° angle.

2. Roll pliers to make small loop.

3. Continue rolling pliers to make spiral.

4. Remove pliers from spiral, move to desired point and change directions.

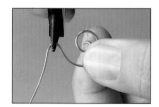

5. Gently roll wire into shape desired.

Crystal Reflections Necklace - MATERIALS: Crystal Assortment glass beads • Crystal Assortment mini glass beads • 4mm Silver beads • 20 gauge Silver wire • Silver crimp beads • Silver barrel clasp • Monofilament • Bead board • Round-nose pliers • Needle-nose pliers • Wire cutters

TIPS: Attach half of barrel clasp to monofilament following instructions on page 3. Make a curly-cue with Silver wire. Choose a large focal bead for dangle. Place focal bead, Silver bead and medium sized Crystal bead on wire curly-cue. Make loop on wire following the instructions on page 6.

String beads for necklace. The beading pattern will make a 16" necklace.

Hold necklace up to see if it is the proper length. Add or remove beads if necessary. Attach barrel clasp to end of necklace. Trim any excess monofilament.

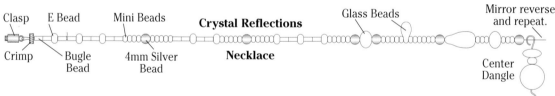

Clasp E Bead Mini Beads **Crystal Reflections** Glass Beads Mirror reverse and repeat.

Crimp Bugle Bead 4mm Silver Bead **Necklace** Center Dangle

Shape Wire

Pink Swirls Necklace - MATERIALS: Pink lampwork beads • Pink Assortment mini glass beads • Amethyst Assortment glass beads • 20 gauge Silver wire • Silver crimp beads • Silver barrel clasp • Tiger tail • Round-nose pliers • Needle-nose pliers • Wire cutters

TIPS: Dangles - Make Silver wire curly-cue. Choose large lampwork focal bead from mix for center dangle and place on curly-cue with seed bead. Make loop on wire following the instructions on page 6. Make 2 identical smaller curly-cues. Place smaller focal beads on curly-cues and make loops.

Determine length of necklace and attach half of barrel clasp to tiger tail following instructions on page 3. String beads following the beading pattern. The pattern will make a 16" necklace with a 1¾" dangle.

Check necklace length. Add or remove beads if necessary. Make mirror image for other side. Attach other half of barrel clasp. Trim any excess tiger tail.

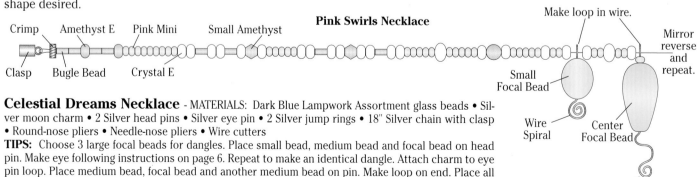

Pink Swirls Necklace

Crimp Amethyst E Pink Mini Small Amethyst Make loop in wire. Mirror reverse and repeat.

Clasp Bugle Bead Crystal E Small Focal Bead

Wire Spiral Center Focal Bead

Celestial Dreams Necklace - MATERIALS: Dark Blue Lampwork Assortment glass beads • Silver moon charm • 2 Silver head pins • Silver eye pin • 2 Silver jump rings • 18" Silver chain with clasp • Round-nose pliers • Needle-nose pliers • Wire cutters

TIPS: Choose 3 large focal beads for dangles. Place small bead, medium bead and focal bead on head pin. Make eye following instructions on page 6. Repeat to make an identical dangle. Attach charm to eye pin loop. Place medium bead, focal bead and another medium bead on pin. Make loop on end. Place all 3 dangles on a large jump ring with charm in center. Attach dangles to center of chain with a jump ring.

Shape Wire

Curly-Cues & Dangles

by Jennifer Mayer

Curly-cues and dangles made from gleaming wire bring a whole new dimension to your jewelry creations!

Blue Dangle Necklace - MATERIALS: Light Blue Assortment glass beads • Matte Crystal E beads or large seed beads • Silver barrel beads • Silver S hook clasp • Decorative head pin • Silver crimp beads • Silver barrel clasp • Jump rings • Tiger tail • Needle-nose pliers
TIPS: Choose a large focal bead for dangle. Thread beads on eye pin. Make loop following the instructions on page 6. Attach dangle to one ring on S hook. Determine length of necklace and attach a barrel clasp to the tiger tail following instructions on page 3.

String beads, alternating size and color to form a pleasing pattern. String a Silver barrel bead approximately every inch. Attach S hook dangle in center.

String remaining beads in mirror image of first half. Attach barrel clasp to end of necklace. Trim excess tiger tail.

Blue Dangle Necklace

Crimp · Trim Tail · Jump ring · S Hook · Mirror reverse and repeat. · Jump ring · Decorative Head Pin · E Beads
Clasp · Glass Bead · Barrel Bead · E Bead · Glass Beads

Moroccan Necklace

Crimp · Spacer Beads · Clasp · Bugle Bead · Mini Glass Bead · Gold Glass Bead · Mirror reverse and repeat. · Glass Beads · Spacer Bead · Head Pin

Amethyst & Silver Jewelry - MATERIALS: Amethyst Assortment glass beads • Amethyst Assortment mini glass beads • Silver spacer beads • 2 Silver flower dangle beads • Decorative head pins • Decorative fishhook earrings • Silver barrel clasp • 2 Silver jump rings • 2 Silver crimp beads • Tiger tail • Needle-nose pliers • Round-nose pliers • Wire cutters • Bead board
TIPS: For necklace, attach clasp to one end of tiger tail, following instructions on page 3. Make dangle on head pin. Continue center until design measures approximately 4".

Follow beading diagram. Hold the necklace up to see if it is the proper length. Add or remove beads if necessary. String mirror image of beads on other side. Attach other half of clasp to end of necklace. Trim excess tiger tail.

Make 2 earrings following diagram. Earrings should be mirror images.

Moroccan Jewelry

MATERIALS: Red Assortment lampwork glass beads • Red Assortment mini glass beads • Silver & Gold Assortment mini glass beads • Gold spacer beads • 3 Gold head pins • Gold crimp beads • Barrel clasp • 4mm Gold jump rings • Gold fishhook earrings • Tiger tail • Round-nose pliers • Needle-nose pliers • Wire cutters • Bead board
TIPS: Choose large focal bead for dangle. Place beads on head pin. Make loop. Determine length of necklace and attach half of barrel clasp to tiger tail.

Place beads for center of necklace on bead board. Add mirror image of pattern on other side of dangle. Center section should measure approximately 6". String beads on tiger tail.

Attach other half of barrel clasp to end of necklace. Trim excess tiger tail.

For each earring, thread beads. Make loop, attach to ear wire with jump ring.

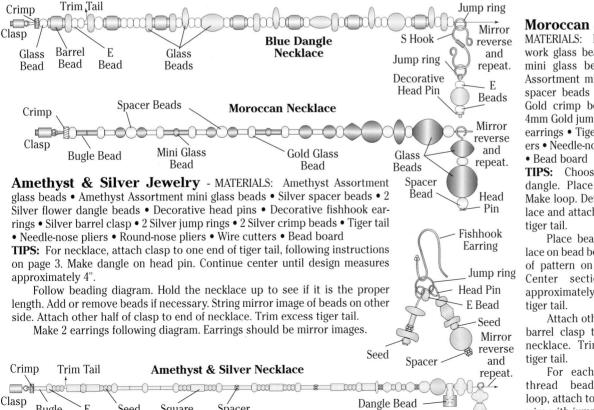

Fishhook Earring · Jump ring · Head Pin · E Bead · Seed · Mirror reverse and repeat. · Seed · Spacer

Amethyst & Silver Necklace
Crimp · Trim Tail · Clasp · Bugle Bead · E Bead · Seed Beads · Square Beads · Spacer Beads · Dangle Bead · Decorative Head Pin

Fishhook Earring · Jump ring · Head Pin · Spacer · Head Pin

Never have enough beads? Try your hand at making a charming beaded chain, then fill the center with dozens of dangles!

by Deb Bergs

Winter Berries Necklace

MATERIALS: Crystal Assortment glass beads • 2 packages of Crystal Assortment mini glass beads • Contrasting accent beads for berries • Size 6° or 8° Crystal seed beads • Sterling Silver clasp • Heavy thread • Needle • Clear nail polish

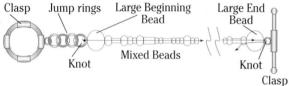

Clasp Jump rings Large Beginning Bead Large End Bead
Knot Mixed Beads Knot Clasp

1. Cut 72" of thread and tie clasp on one end. Select 2 large matching beads and run thread through first bead. Pour rest of the smaller and larger beads into a bowl and mix with 6° or 8° seed beads. String 20" of beads on thread, being sure to add a large bead every 1½" to 2". Knot to other end of clasp.

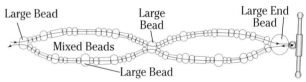

Large Bead Large Bead Large End Bead
Mixed Beads Large Bead

2. Run thread back through large bead. and string 1" to 2" of beads. Go through a large bead on the previous row.

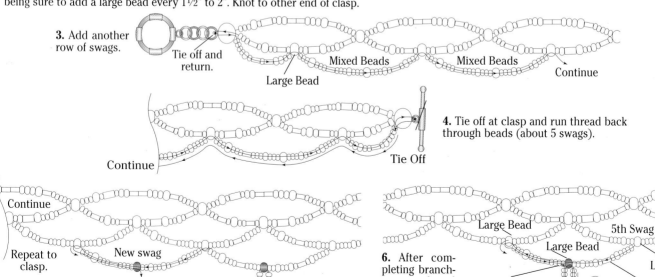

3. Add another row of swags.
Tie off and return.
Large Bead Mixed Beads Mixed Beads Continue

Continue Tie Off

4. Tie off at clasp and run thread back through beads (about 5 swags).

Continue
Repeat to clasp. New swag Make branch dangle.

5. Make one swag, run thread through large bead and seed bead on previous row. Return thread to center of swag just made and add branches following diagram.

6. After completing branches, run thread through swag and add new swag. Continue adding swags and branches
Large Bead 5th Swag
Large Bead Large Bead
Return through large bead and repeat. Mixed Beads
Make branch dangles.

on center section of necklace (about 4"). Run thread through previous row to end. Tie off.

Glasses Holders

Make beaded eyeglasses holders casual enough to wear to the office and elegant enough for the opera!

by Carole Rodgers

Eyeglass Necklaces - MATERIALS: Size #10 beading needle • Round-nose pliers • Scissors • Bead sorting dishes • Gem-Tac Permanent Adhesive

MATERIALS FOR AUTUMN NECKLACE: Autumn Assortment glass beads • Gold 11° seed beads • Gold eyeglass holders • 2 Gold clamshell bead tips • Brown beading thread

MATERIALS FOR SEA BREEZE NECKLACE: Sea Breeze Assortment glass beads • 16 Silver beads • Size 11° seed beads • Silver eyeglass holders • 2 Silver clamshell bead tips • Blue beading thread

TIPS: For Autumn Necklace, double thread needle with 80" of thread. Tie waste seed bead at very end, glue knot and trim ends of thread. Pass through a clamshell bead tip and close tip carefully around seed bead.

Sort beads into piles. Place individual beads in a separate place. Be sure you have an even number of matching beads and divide them into 2 dishes. Pour out some Gold seed beads as well. Thread Gold seed bead then randomly select larger beads. Continue alternating seed beads with larger beads until you have 14", end with a Gold seed bead. Pick out several individual beads you removed earlier and make dangle. Thread beads for dangle starting and ending with Gold seed. Skip last seed and pass back through beads. Pick up Gold seed and thread other side of necklace being sure to thread a mirror image of first side. Finish by taking needle through clamshell tip and tying off against waste seed bead. Close clamshell and attach each to an eyeglass holder.

NOTE: You might find it beneficial to attach a clasp and tag to the clamshell tip with jump ring as well as the eyeglass holders. You can use the necklace with the tassel in the front if you don't want to wear it for an eyeglass holder.

For Sea Breeze Necklace, sort Blue and Silver beads. Double thread needle with 80" of thread and attach clamshell tip. Thread beads following diagram. Starting with a seed bead reverse the order of beads and string other side. Finish by tying off against a waste seed bead in clamshell tip. Attach clamshells to eyeglass holders.

Autumn Dangle

Glass Beads
Seed Beads
Glass
Glass
Glass
Seed
Glass
Seed
Glass

Clamshell Bead Tip

Waste Seed Bead

Close clamshell and begin beading.

Knot, trim & glue.

Seed Bead

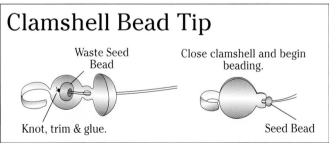

Seed Bead   Glass Bead   **Sea Breeze Necklace**

Eyeglass Holder   Clamshell Bead Tip   Silver Bead   Silver Bead

Continue pattern until you have 8 Silver beads.

8th Silver Bead

Mirror image and repeat.

Make Dangle

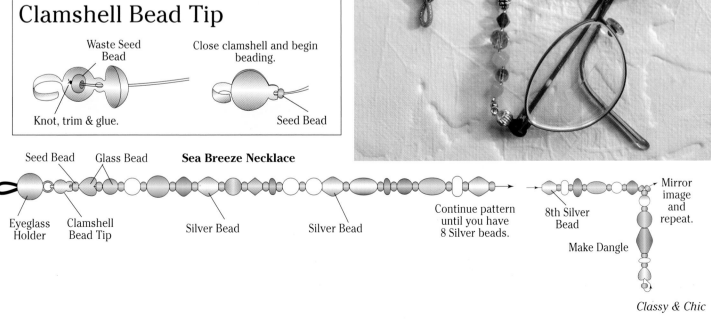

Pulls, Braids & Expansion Bracelets

by Carole Rodgers

Zipper Pulls - MATERIALS: 6 to 10 beads for each pull (assorted metal, glass bead, seed) • 8" of Beadalon 19-strand beading wire • Clamshell bead tip • Split ring or jump ring • Lobster claw clasp • Crimp bead • Wire cutters • Needle-nose pliers • Round-nose pliers
TIPS: Pick large bead and several smaller beads that complement or contrast with large bead. Arrange beads in a pleasing pattern with heaviest bead toward bottom. Refer to the photo.

Thread seed bead on one 8" piece of wire and center. Place ends together and use both to thread remaining beads. Thread 2 smaller beads after seed bead. Next thread large bead and remaining beads in decreasing size. Take wire ends through clamshell from bottom. Crimp wires together. Trim wire ends and close clam shell. Attach clamshell to split ring or jump ring, attach to clasp. Attach the clasp to zipper.

Expandable Winter Beads Bracelet - MATERIALS: 2 packages of Winter Assortment glass beads • Seed beads in matching colors • Two row expandable bracelet • 126 Silver 2" or 2½" head pins • Needle-nose pliers • Round-nose pliers • Wire cutters • Bead sorting dishes
TIPS: Pour Winter beads into dish. Pour seed beads in second dish. This bracelet is entirely random selection. Pick up seed bead on head pin, then Winter bead and another seed. Bend head pin above second seed. Trim pin to ³⁄₈" and make loop. Repeat for all pins. If you need more dangles, use excess that you cut off. Turn one end into a loop, thread on beads and make loop on other end. Randomly use these with other beaded pins. Attach 2 dangles to bottom loop and one to top. On next section reverse order and alternate around bracelet. If you want a fuller look, attach 2 dangles to each of the loops.

Multiple Strand Necklace - MATERIALS: Jet Assortment mini glass beads • Crystal Assortment mini glass beads • Black and White Nymo D beading thread • Size 10 beading needle • 3-strand Silver clasp • 6 Silver clamshell bead tips • Round-nose pliers • Scissors • Bead sorting dish • Gem-Tac Permanent Adhesive
TIPS: Pour Crystal beads into dish. Double thread needle with 48" of White thread. Double knot waste seed bead at the end and thread clamshell tip from inside (see page 15). Randomly thread Crystal beads until you have 19". Pass through clamshell tip from bottom and tie on waste seed bead. Repeat to make 3 strands.

Pour out Jet beads. Double thread needle with 48" of Black thread. Tie to starting seed bead in one Crystal strand and pass through the clamshell tip. Thread 19" of beads. Twist strands together, pass through clamshell and tie off. Be sure both ends are securely knotted. Glue knots, trim thread ends and close clamshells. Repeat for other 2 strands. Attach clamshell to one end of clasp with round-nose pliers. Pin clasp to a solid surface. Braid twisted strands loosely until you reach opposite end. Attach clamshells to clasp.

Expandable Bracelet

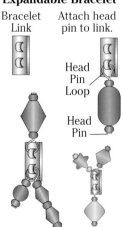

Bracelet Link   Attach head pin to link.

Head Pin Loop

Head Pin

Attach 2 head pins to bottom and 1 to top. Alternate dangles.

From zipper pulls to an expansion bracelet to an intricate looking braided necklace, you're sure to find a project you love!

Eye Beads

Keep a fresh eye on the world with a necklace and earrings featuring gorgeous handmade beads!

by Carole Rodgers

Eye Beads Set - MATERIALS: 9 assorted color 12mm eye beads • 18 Black E beads • Black seed beads • Gold toggle clasp • 2 Gold clamshell bead tips • 2 Gold 2" head pins • Gold ball and loop earrings • 3 yards of Black beading thread • 2 size 10 beading needles • Scissors • Wire cutters • Needle-nose pliers • Round-nose pliers • Bead sorting dish • Gem-Tac Permanent Adhesive

TIPS: Use 2 Needle Right Angle Weave. Place needle on each end of beading thread keeping thread even on both needles. Thread on one Black seed bead and center. Take both needles through clamshell bead tip. Close clamshell gently around seed bead. On each needle, pick up 2 seed beads. Pick up third on one needle and pass second needle through this bead from opposite direction. Pull threads snug against clamshell. Continue until you have 27 rectangles.

Pass both needles through E, eye and E beads for an eye bead unit. Add 7 eye bead units spaced apart with 9 seed bead rectangles. Finish necklace with 27 seed bead rectangles.

Take both needles through clamshell from bottom. Thread seed bead on one needle. Push into clamshell tip. Tie off threads against bead. Glue knot and trim threads. Close clamshell. Attach clamshells to toggle clasp.

For earrings, thread seed, E, eye, E and seed bead on head pins. Bend head pins at right angle, trim to ⅜" and make loop with round-nose pliers. Attach loops to earrings.

Eye Beads Necklace

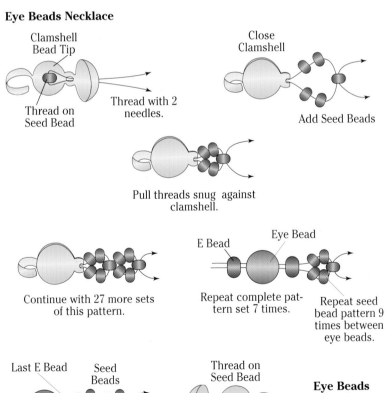

Clamshell Bead Tip

Thread on Seed Bead

Thread with 2 needles.

Close Clamshell

Add Seed Beads

Pull threads snug against clamshell.

Continue with 27 more sets of this pattern.

E Bead

Eye Bead

Repeat complete pattern set 7 times.

Repeat seed bead pattern 9 times between eye beads.

Last E Bead   Seed Beads

Repeat pattern for 27 sets.

Thread on Seed Bead

End by passing both needles through the bottom of clamshell. Thread seed bead on one needle. Push into clamshell tip. Tie off threads against bead. Glue knot and trim threads. Attach to clasp.

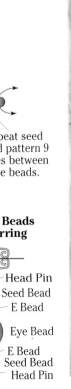

Eye Beads Earring

Head Pin
Seed Bead
E Bead

Eye Bead

E Bead
Seed Bead
Head Pin

Symphonies in Blue

Ask anyone, "What's your favorite color?" and the most likely answer is blue! Make a dangle-filled necklace or a memory wire cuff bracelet for a sure-to-please gift!

by Carole Rodgers

Blue Branches Necklace - MATERIALS: Light Blue Assortment glass beads • Blue E beads • Blue 11° seed beads • Silver Lobster claw clasp and tag • 2 Silver 4mm jump rings • 2 Silver clamshell bead tips • 10 yards of Blue Nymo D beading thread • Size 10 beading needle • Scissors • Round-nose pliers • Bead sorting dishes • Gem-Tac Permanent Adhesive

TIPS: Double thread needle with 60" of thread. Slip on seed bead and tie double knot at end of thread around bead leaving a few inches of thread tail. Pass needle through a clamshell tip from inside.

Thread Blue E beads to desired length. The sample is about 22" long. Take needle through second clamshell from bottom. Tie off thread against seed bead. Trim thread to few inches and let hang.

Cut new thread at least 5 times length of necklace and single thread needle. Go through first seed bead and first clamshell tip pulling thread through until you leave 4" tail. Tie 4" end of new thread very securely around seed bead and to first thread. Trim thread ends, glue knot and close clamshell tip carefully.

Pass needle through first 7 or 8 E beads in necklace. Come out and pick up 5 or 6 seed beads then large bead and another seed. Skip last seed bead and go back through other beads pulling thread tight. Pass needle back into necklace and come out 3 or 4 beads down necklace. Repeat process. Vary length of 'branches' and larger beads and colors. You can use more than one large bead.

If you are running out of thread, take needle and thread through necklace to other end and tie off against seed bead in other end. Start a new thread from first end and take it through necklace to place where you left off and continue. When finished, leave about 7 beads at the end. Pass needle through second clamshell tip and tie off, glue and close clamshell. Use round-nose pliers to make loops in clamshells and attach to clasp and tag with jump rings.

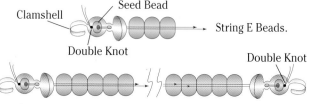

String E beads to desired length and tie off at other end.

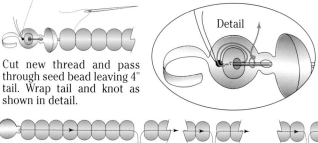

Cut new thread and pass through seed bead leaving 4" tail. Wrap tail and knot as shown in detail.

Detail

E Beads

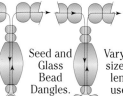

Continue thread through 7 or 8 E beads. Make dangle. Pass needle back into necklace and come out 3 or 4 beads down necklace. Repeat.

Seed and Glass Bead Dangles.

Vary bead sizes and lengths used in dangles.